Eating Disorders

Phyllis and James Alsdurf

InterVarsity Press® is the book-publishing division of InterVarsity Christian Fellowship®, a student movement active on campus at hundreds of universities, colleges and schools of nursing in the United States of America, and a member movement of the International Fellowship of Evangelical Students. For information about local and regional activities, write Public Relations Dept., InterVarsity Christian Fellowship, 6400 Schroeder Rd., P.O. Box 7895, Madison, WI 53707-7895.

All Scripture quotations, unless otherwise indicated, are taken from the HOLY BIBLE, NEW INTERNATIONAL VERSION®. NIV®. Copyright ©1973, 1978, 1984 by International Bible Society. Used by permission of Zondervan Publishing House. All rights reserved.

The opening story, by Yvonne Sybring, appeared in its original form in FreeWay and was reprinted in HIS magazine, ©1983.

The closing story, by Carol Anderson, first appeared in Steps and is used by permission of the author.

ISBN 0-87784-091-1

Printed in the United States of America ∞

| 14 | 13 | 12 | 11 | 10 | 9 | 8 | 7 | 6 | 5 | 4 | 3 | 2 |
| 03 | 02 | 01 | 00 | 99 | | | | | | | | |

At seventeen I was supposedly a model kid—with good grades, a nice home, great parents and many friends. I should have been enjoying life, but I seemed bent on ending it all.

The seeds of my nightmare had been sown long before. As a little girl I was taught that it was not acceptable to express negative emotions like anger. My parents were strict and had high standards for me, standards I tried my best to live up to. But as I got older I began to feel powerless, like everything was outside of my control.

The summer I turned sixteen things got worse. Working at a resort for two months, I watched in despair as my weight climbed from 118 to 140 pounds. When I came home I hated the way looked. At a family reunion my dad remarked that I was "filling out." I became obsessed with losing weight, and within months my obsession was out of control.

Summer arrived again, and I returned to the resort. But this time, instead of overeating, I exercised like a maniac and ate like a bird. By the time I came home I was little more than a walking scarecrow. In eight months I had gone from 140 to 87 pounds. I had developed anorexia nervosa. The idea of eating, of gaining even an ounce, terrified me. At the same time I felt a certain sense of power in not eating. My parents frantically tried to force me to eat. But when no amount of scolding, threatening, pleading or crying could persuade me to put food in my stomach, they realized that something was dreadfully wrong.

They watched as I grew sullen, irritable and fearful. My bones began to protrude. My hair fell out. The only emotion I felt was self-hatred. I begged God to let me die. I'll just vanish, just fade into the air, I thought.

———————

"You can't be too thin. To be thin is to be beautiful, smart, accepted and in control." That message screams out at us from the TV screen, the billboards, the magazines lining the grocery check-out stand.

Coupled with it is the idea that food is the ultimate reward. It is turned to for comfort or as a substitute for love, friendship or success. The same magazine that sports pencil-thin beauties on its cover features pages of sumptuous-looking desserts within.

Out of just such a cultural setting has arisen a duet of eating disorders—anorexia nervosa and bulimia nervosa. The number of victims has risen dramatically in recent years. Anorexia nervosa is deliberate self-starvation. Bulimia nervosa involves bingeing on food and then purging through regurgitation, laxatives and diuretics. While an estimated 90 to 95 percent of the victims of anorexia and bulimia are female, a growing number of men are also afflicted. Recent studies have found that a large number of bulimics have been victims of physical and sexual abuse, rape or battering.

Bulimia and anorexia are special problems for young women who have been taught to be dependent, unassertive and passive and not to express anger. Anorexics and bulimics tend to look to others for their needs to be met and define themselves externally—by their appearance, their achievements or what others think of them. Some come from abusive families or from homes which are rigidly perfectionistic. As both bulimia and anorexia develop they lead to increased emotional withdrawal and rigidity. A woman's obsessiveness about food increases as her self-esteem and self-identity erode.

Does this sound like someone you know—or you? Then it is important to realize a hidden truth here: *Food is not the main issue with either of these disorders.* They are but two different means of indicating that something is wrong psychologically. Unfortunately, because the psychological symptoms—depression, low self-esteem, hypersensitivity, social withdrawal and isolation—are exacerbated by starvation, what results over time is a complex intertwining of physical and psychological problems. It is also not uncommon for women with these eating disorders to abuse drugs, alcohol or diet pills, to shoplift in order to obtain money for binge-eating, or to attempt suicide because of the emotional and physical chaos of their lives.

Anorexia Nervosa

Anorexics are primarily young women in adolescence and early adulthood who are highly sensitive and compulsive and suffer from low self-esteem. Roughly 10 percent of all anorexics die—half from suicide and half from anorexia-related complications. The anorexic commonly is defined as a person whose body weight is 25 percent lower than normal for her height and age. In extreme cases she may have the emaciated look of a concentration camp survivor. Because of her distorted body image, the anorexic looks in the mirror critically and sees someone who is not "perfect," someone who still has weight to lose. She has ceased to menstruate, her hair has become thin and dull, her teeth are more susceptible to decay and erosion, and she is a likely candidate for a variety of physical side effects from her starvation: kidney problems, cardiac arrest, muscle spasms, swollen salivary glands, bloating and urinary difficulties.

The typical anorexic is a young, white female from a middle- to upper-middle-class family in which high achievement and perfection have been emphasized. Often she has been a "model child," eager to please her parents and teachers and well liked by her peers. Anorexia may first develop at some point of separation such as during puberty or as a reaction to the death of a loved one. It also may emerge in response to an earlier trauma—childhood sexual molestation or abuse, for instance. An underlying theme for the anorexic is a fear of intimate relationships. While on the surface she may look happy and well-adjusted, the anorexic is actually fearful, insecure and driven by perfectionistic tendencies. She is a child who has learned to suppress negative feelings and anger, one who is overly compliant and eager to please others. Living in an environment where success and attainment are emphasized, she is plagued by feelings of unworthiness and power-lessness.

The anorexic's family often appears to be warm

and loving yet in reality may be unable to tolerate open expression of conflict. In some situations, family members are too dependent upon one another or are overly involved in each other's lives (opening other's personal mail, entering closed rooms without knocking). Or the home environment may be one in which parents are emotionally unavailable or in which an atmosphere of intimidation prevails. Victims of anorexia often have been given special advantages and generally have performed up to their parents' expectations socially, academically and athletically. Consequently, they may be afraid to admit that there is anything wrong at home.

Initially the anorexic may diet in order to lose five or ten pounds. In the beginning of her weight loss, friends and family often praise her for her hard work in dieting. What is not apparent is that the dieting regimen has provided the anorexic with a sense of power and control she has not previously experienced. In a world where control always has come from outside of herself, externally established by those with authority over her, sticking to a rigid diet gives the anorexic a personal sense of victory, a feeling of power and superiority over those around her.

About half of all anorexics also engage in regurgitation as a way of ridding the body of unwanted food. Many compulsively smoke cigarettes or drink coffee and caffeinated soda. Others use laxatives and diuretics, drugs that increase the body's production of urine, to further purge their bodies of water weight. In addition to absolutely rigid dieting standards, anorexics generally participate in chronic exercise and have a fear of sitting still. Some are not even able to sleep for fear of putting on weight. When vigorous exercise is added to dieting and purging, the physical condition soon begins to deteriorate.

Eventually the anorexic becomes totally preoccupied with food, calories and nutrition. She often adopts strange eating habits and rituals and may be obsessed with cooking, fad diets and nutrition while refusing to eat herself. It is not uncommon for anorexics to develop other obsessive-compulsive behaviors as well, such as compulsions about cleanliness and organization.

Tension eventually emerges in the family when parents insist that their child gain weight, try to tantalize her with elaborately prepared meals, compare her to other children or blame themselves for her problems. Very often they fail to see any correlation between the atmosphere in the home and their daughter's slow suicide by starvation. As the condition persists, family members become increasingly frustrated over the anorexic's inability to make an emotional connection with anyone. They may give up in despair and try to ignore her odd, obsessional behaviors.

From the anorexic's perspective, however, the eating disorder brings her a level of recognition and validation from her family which she has not before experienced. "Receiving recognition and having my parents show concern was what I wanted," said one recovered anorexic. "It made me feel special. Unfortunately, I only thought I was special when I was underweight."

"The anorectic cannot tolerate feelings," says Susie Orbach in *Hunger Strike*. "She gathers strength from the knowledge that she can ignore her needs and appetites. . . . On the one hand anorexia is about being thin—very, very thin. It is an expression of a woman's confusion about how much space she may take up in the world. On the other hand, her food denial is driven by the need to control her body which is, for her, a symbol of emotional needs. If she can get control over her body, then perhaps she can similarly control her emotional neediness. Submitting her body to rigorous discipline is part of her attempt to deny an emotional life."

Because the anorexic is a person who has not developed her own sense of identity, the anorexia itself soon becomes her identity. Without it she fears that she will no longer exist.

———————

I learned early on that it wasn't okay to be myself, to actually say what I thought. On the surface my family looked great. My parents were Christians; they were involved in the church. But everything we did was done in order to keep up appearances. There was a lot of secret-keeping and the church seemed to buy into that. I felt like I was dying inside.

As far back as grade school I can remember this obsession with not getting fat. The focus in my family was not on eating something because it was good for you, but always on not eating, so you wouldn't gain weight. It built a fear in me that I would be fat and also the understanding that if I could just be thin, then I would be acceptable.

When I was sixteen I was a bit pudgy and my mother repeatedly expressed concern over my weight. The idea was that if you really wanted to be thin, you could do it. The message I got from church was that if there was something wrong in your life you just had to turn it over to Jesus and then everything would be okay.

By the time I was out of high school and looking ahead to college, I was starving myself for a week and then bingeing. Then I started purging by vomiting. In addition, I kept up a frantic exercise program—preparing for marathons, working out two to three hours a day.

Fifteen years later I was finally ready to admit that I had an eating disorder. I had a complete obsession with food. I was bingeing and purging three to four times a day. Finally, after I broke up with my boyfriend, I entered *an outpatient program at an area hospital. Before that, I could never really admit I had an eating disorder. I took a leave from work and for three weeks spent all day in the outpatient program. My recovery has taken several years but I am no longer plagued by an eating disorder.*

My bulimia was really a form of rebelling against the world around me, I guess. It was either that or losing myself. In some sense, it kept me from dying inside.

I don't blame my parents for my eating disorder, but they taught me not to say what I thought. They correlated choosing the safe way with the Christian faith. What I've experienced is that the safe way doesn't seem to be God's way. It's often just another word for denial.

Bulimia Nervosa

Bulimia nervosa involves a cycle of dieting, bingeing (eating huge amounts of food) and purging. Rarely heard of before the 1960s, bulimia now is believed to affect 3 percent of American women between the ages of 14 and 40. Studies indicate that up to 35 percent of all women on college campuses have engaged in some form of bingeing and purging. An estimated 7.6 million women claim to have binged and purged at some point in their lives. Celebrities such as Princess Diana and Jane Fonda are among those who have revealed their struggles with bulimia and raised public awareness of this hidden disorder.

Bulimics may first use purging as a means of relieving the guilt of having binged on food. The bingeing and subsequent purging might begin as a group activity, perhaps in a college dorm as a way of "pigging out" without having to pay for it with added pounds. For some women, however, the purging soon becomes a pattern, a method of dealing with conflict or covering up emotional pain; at that point the purging takes control.

The bingeing/purging syndrome soon becomes integrated into a woman's lifestyle and embedded into her pattern of dealing with emotional tension. It becomes a comforting behavior, one she turns to under stress or when facing emotional conflict. Many women with this disorder have been sexually abused or assaulted. Self-starvation and purging are ways to deal with that trauma or relieve feelings of shame, rage, terror and vulnerability.

Bulimics tend to look healthier than anorexics because they maintain a normal body weight. However, binge eating followed by vomiting or purging through the use of laxatives and diuretics can have devastating long-term effects. Repeated vomiting deprives the body of essential minerals and fluids and can lead to the inability to swallow normally. Bulimics often suffer from persisting sore throats, and their teeth are susceptible to decay and deterioration or staining caused by stomach acids.

As the pattern persists, the bulimic organizes more and more of her life around bingeing and purging. Her bulimia becomes the focal point of her day, yet it remains a secret, one which increases her sense of isolation and shame.

Like the anorexic, the bulimic generally comes from a family in which success and ambition are emphasized. Parents are frequently preoccupied with work, demanding high levels of performance from their daughter and yet emotionally distant from her. Her family often stresses physical appearance. In some situations the mother pressures her daughter to achieve the career success she never had.

While the bulimic has daily periods of emotional chaos at the point of her bingeing and purging, overall her life appears productive and organized. She may have rigid behavioral patterns with relationship to her eating, purging and elimination, but the rest of her existence appears normal. Consequently, her eating disorder can exist for many years before family members are even aware of it. For the bulimic, the urge to binge is a signal that there is some internal state that needs attention. Bulimics generally avoid expressing anger for fear of rejection. The bingeing and purging become a method of dealing with anxiety and depression.

Treating the Eating Disorder

Both bulimics and anorexics use food as an avenue to express deeper emotional needs. A central issue with both disorders is *control*. A young girl or woman who feels powerless or feels that things are chaotic and "out of control" in her life may use food (bingeing or starvation) as a means of exerting some control over her life. For the anorexic, emotional starvation has preceded the physical starvation. Among other things, recovery will require learning self-acceptance and appropriate methods of dealing with feelings.

Anorexia is a difficult disorder to treat because the patient really believes she is fat. Likewise, because bulimia can persist for many years without being detected, deep patterns of bingeing and purging can become integrated into the woman's lifestyle, making treatment especially difficult. The shorter the duration of the disorder and the younger the patient at the time of treatment, the better the chances of recovery.

The first step in getting help is to admit that a problem exists. If you recognize yourself in the descriptions above, please stop hiding your problem. Seek help from a doctor or therapist experienced in dealing with eating disorders. Hospitals in most major cities have special inpatient and outpatient treatment programs specifically designed for those with eating disorders. Many women with eating disorders have benefited from programs such as those offered through Overeaters Anonymous.

For severe anorexia, hospitalization may be required until the patient is nutritionally stable. Treatment is rarely undertaken by the patient willingly, and it is not uncommon for her to have several relapses after being released from a treatment program. It is important that a program be staffed by those skilled in treating eating disorders so that the patient can get qualified care which deals not only with symptoms but with underlying problems as well.

Trying to Help

What can you do if you suspect that your friend or sister has an eating disorder? There is no one "right" way to approach a person you suspect of being bulimic or anorexic. In general, it is best to be forthright about your concern—but expect some hostility. Rather than stating that your friend looks "too thin" (which may only be taken as a compliment), discuss ways in which perfectionism and need for control have affected your relationship.

Be honest about what you have observed or suspect (quantities of food missing from the cupboards, frequent vomiting, meals skipped) and don't couch what you say in vague, nonoffensive terms so as not to embarrass your friend. Her disorder needs to be addressed openly, yet in such a way as to not increase her own sense of shame and guilt.

Be prepared to offer specific suggestions about where the anorexic or bulimic can get help and to accompany her to appointments in order to ensure that she follows through on any promises. But be careful not to get into a power struggle with her. Remember, *the issue is control.* Expect that your intervention will result in anger and denial.

Anorexics and bulimics are likely to refuse help, primarily because they do believe that they are intolerably fat, they eat too much or they exercise too little. Despite how much they may protest and disagree, they need to be confronted with the danger and reality of what they are doing to themselves.

Don't expect that your initial confrontation will result in immediate action. Try to see beyond feelings of anger and betrayal and continue to express your concerns while respecting your friend's right to make decisions about her own life. Firm and consistent "reality testing" from those around her—especially if it can come from several sources (roommates, family members, doctors)—will set the stage for her eventual decision to seek professional help.

In some extreme situations, emergency intervention is necessary and must be taken without delay. Such is the case when there is the possibility of suicide, when the person has passed out or is too weak to walk and when there is the likelihood of death due to starvation. The bulimic or anorexic probably will not willingly cooperate even under these severe conditions; you must persevere and do whatever is necessary to see that she gets immediate medical help.

For specific information about anorexia and

bulimia, as well as lists of support groups, treatment programs and therapists specializing in eating disorders in your area, contact the National Association of Anorexia Nervosa and Associated Disorders or one of the other organizations listed in the back of this booklet.

———————————

I was a competitive athlete from about age seven through college and was training for the Olympics as a swimmer. I have a driven type of personality and have always been highly motivated to achieve.

In my family you didn't discuss emotions at all. Appearances were very important. My mother is thin and attractive and I was always intimidated by that. I wasn't allowed to express negative emotions. I ignored them for years and years, and they finally came out in the form of an eating disorder.

I always thought of myself as being better when I was thinner. But it wasn't until I was in law school that I really started having problems. I was insecure about where I was and what I was doing. I lost fifteen pounds the first year. I was working out twice a day and was making myself vomit as well. I knew it was wrong, but I couldn't control it. That created guilt which put a wedge in my relationship with God.

I went through a twelve-step program for Christians with eating disorders, but it didn't help. I wasn't ready to face the fact that I was trying to be something God didn't intend me to be. I'm not a 110-pound person and I wasn't intended to be one. I had to come to the point where I would turn that over to God. I had to relinquish control of something I wanted very much.

I was the only Christian in my family, and I felt I had to be perfect in my faith. When I went to see a counselor it seemed like an admission of failure, because in my family it's unheard of to talk to someone about your feelings.

In dealing with my eating disorder I've had to face my need for forgiveness. I'd always been a good kid, a great athlete, never openly rebelled, but my Christianity was a "works" thing. I never really understood my need for forgiveness. Now I know that Christ is the One who is perfect for us. God loves us just as we are. His love is unconditional.

Eating Disorders and the Christian

Christian women are not immune to eating disorders. In fact, for some, a distorted understanding of what the Bible teaches with regard to self-control and fighting temptation only supports their obsessiveness about not eating. Others are plagued with guilt and believe that they cannot overcome their struggle with anorexia or bulimia because they do not "have enough faith."

If you are anorexic or bulimic, please know that healing is possible. Of course, it will not come instantaneously. You too will need to discover what hurts you have been burying under mounds of food, what inner needs you have ignored and sublimated, what the roots of your sense of shame and self-hatred are. Even the act of admitting you have an eating disorder can be a tremendously painful step because it means a relinquishing of the little bit of control you have and a giving up of pride. It takes courage to admit you are in need of help.

An important part of the healing process is learning new ways of identifying and expressing your feelings. As you come to really understand the depth of Christ's acceptance and forgiveness of you, it will be easier to forgive others (your parents, boyfriends, other people) and to accept yourself for who you are. Learning appropriate ways of asserting yourself will also come gradually and help give you a healthy sense of control over your life.

The inner void which you feel must be filled with a new sense of identity. While that identity is rooted in your relationship with Christ, it will no doubt also involve a reevaluation of your view of God. Many Christian bulimics and anorexics have perceived God as harsh and unloving, someone, like their earthly parents, with a long list of "shoulds" who is never pleased with their efforts.

If you struggle with an eating disorder, be assured that God's love, his forgiveness and his deliverance are available to *you*. He can heal the pain which causes you to engage in self-destructive behavior and help you see that you are acceptable and treasured just as you are by a loving God who protects you from shame.

Healing from the self-destructiveness of anorexia or bulimia means facing the self-rejection which is at its core. That perspective must be reconciled with the truth of Scripture—that each person has been "fearfully and wonderfully made" (Ps 139:13-14), that the body itself is God's temple and sacred (1 Cor 3:16-17; 6:19-20), that God offers deliverance from fears and that those who look to him "are never covered with shame" (Ps 34:5).

This process will take months and even years to complete as old patterns are dismantled and healthy ones constructed. It involves a "renewing of the mind" so that the pressure to conform to the "patterns of this world" (Rom 12:2)—patterns which idealize being thin as the epitome of power, control and beauty—can be withstood and conquered.

———————

I was twenty-two years old, stood five feet eight inches tall and weighed ninety-four pounds. For almost four years I had been experiencing the bewildering downward spiral into bulimia and anorexia nervosa. I was lonely. I was frightened. I was vomiting up to ten times a day and didn't know if there was a way out of the madness. I felt as if I were in a very dark tunnel.

To all outward appearances, I was a bright, attractive, fun-loving go-getter. Down under, I was the little girl who believed if she could just be perfect she would be lovable. The bulimia/anorexia began to manifest itself my freshman year in college. At 94 pounds I finally confessed to a compassionate school nurse the hell I was living. I was hospitalized briefly and had counseling. I hovered between 105 and 110 for several years and by the grace of God was able to do graduate work and get a job. I still binged at least twice a day and struggled with feelings of hypocrisy and guilt.

Three years ago I went to the bulimia/anorexia chapter of Overeaters Anonymous. When the meeting started, I looked around the room disbelieving. Here were slim, attractive professional women who said they were eating three meals a day and not bingeing or purging anymore. I desperately wanted what they had. I had let this thing control my life for so long. This time I decided I would do whatever it took to be well. I would risk gaining weight. I told God I would do whatever I had to do and asked for his help to do it. That was the beginning.

I went to meetings and got a sponsor. I was accountable to her for what I ate and I called her when I was struggling with compulsions. It took me two weeks before I could get through a whole day without bingeing. I had been a bulimic for ten years. The habit was deeply ingrained. I had used food as my response to life: to numb pain, to deal with joy, to ease loneliness and to fill that everlasting hole of the need to be loved.

God's healing power was real and available to me when I took the responsibility to make choices of action toward becoming well. With each risk I took, I found a strength and courage far beyond what I had known in earlier days when I had begged God to do my work for me. I also came to realize that God loved me completely for who I was, whether I was bingeing or not. With this growing sense of complete acceptance, I found the hole inside beginning to fill. For me, it took that foundation of acceptance to come to love myself.

My journey into health has been a gradual, painful and yet surprisingly beautiful process. There have been times when I've failed. But I have never let it stop me from pursuing my goal. I was determined to become well. And I had no idea of the harvest of good things that would come once I stopped bingeing and purging. Not *only did my limbs fill out, but my whole person as well.*

I went through a period of rage and grief. I'm still in the process of forgiving my parents and learning to love them in a new way. But I have come to the point where I know that with God's power and my responsible choices, I can be completely healed of bulimia/anorexia. I've come out of the tunnel, and I'm dancing in the light.

Resources

Books

Allender, Dan B. *The Wounded Heart.* Colorado Springs, Colo.: NavPress, 1990.

Black, Claudia. *Double Duty.* New York: Ballantine, 1990.

Bray-Garretson, Helen, and Kaye V. Cook. *Chaotic Eating.* Grand Rapids, Mich.: Zondervan, 1992.

Bruch, Hilde. *The Golden Cage: The Enigma of Anorexia Nervosa.* Cambridge, Mass.: Harvard University Press, 1978.

Levenkron, Steven. *Obsessive Compulsive Disorders.* New York: Warner, 1991.

Orbach, Susie. *Hunger Strike.* New York: Avon, 1986.

Remuda Ranch. *Beyond the Looking Glass: Daily Devotions for Overcoming Anorexia and Bulimia.*

Nashville: Nelson, 1992.

Siegel, Michelle, Judith Brisman and Margot Weinshel. *Surviving an Eating Disorder: Strategies for Family and Friends.* New York: Harper & Row, 1988.

Organizations

American Anorexia/Bulimia Association, Inc.
133 Cedar Lane
Teaneck, NJ 07666
201-836-1800

Anorexia Nervosa and Associated Disorders
(ANAD)
P.O. Box 7
Highland Park, IL 60035
312-831-3438

Anorexia Nervosa and Related Eating Disorders,
Inc.
P.O. Box 5102
Eugene, OR 97405
503-344-1144

National Anorexia Aid Society Inc. (NAAS)
5796 Karl Road
Columbus, OH 43229
614-895-2009

Center for the Study of Anorexia and Bulimia
1 West 91st Street
New York, NY 10028
212-595-3449

Overeaters Anonymous
Check local listings.

Phyllis Alsdurf is a writer and the former editor of Family Life Today *magazine. James Alsdurf (Ph.D.) is a clinical psychologist for the Bureau of Community Corrections in Hennepin County, Minnesota.*